A Testament to Life & Death

Peter deGraft-Johnson: The Repeat Beat Poet

VERVE
POETRY PRESS
BIRMINGHAM

PUBLISHED BY VERVE POETRY PRESS
https://vervepoetrypress.com
mail@vervepoetrypress.com

FIRST PUBLISHED FEB 2022

Printed and bound in the UK
by Positive Print, Birmingham

ISBN: 978-1-913917-04-3

I

For The Poets	7
Aretha & Grace	9
The Faithful	10
I Haven't Written Honestly Since They Started Banning Drill	12
Swinging	14

II

Once I Get Out Of Bed	17
Black View	18
Desecrated	20
Can't Stop Won't Stop	21
Memoriam For A Fallen Pear	23
Sick With Weight	24

III

Seeping	26
Heavy Footsteps In Snow	27
Tommy Builds A Cocktail	29
What Does Black Power Mean?	30
Beware The Vicar's Daughter	32
A Step-By-Step Guide To Saving 'The British Dream'	34

IV

One Black Lotus (For William Davidson)	36
Cocoon Cracks	38
Resurvival	40
Discovering Poems Through Observation And Elimination	41

Acknowledgements

*In dedication to, and in jubilant memory of
the ones who raised the ones that raised me*

*Sarah Amoah
Francis Ignatius Human Baffour
Josephine Maria deGraft-Johnson (aka Mother)
George Kuntu Blankson (aka GKB, Paa George)*

*Rev. Joseph William deGraft-Johnson
Alice deGraft-Johnson
Eva Coleman Daniels*

and for Dean McKee

A Testament to Life & Death

I

Dedications
(For Nipsey Hussle)

For The Poets

This is for those fleeting moment capturers that enrapture us
For the rhyme flingers and wordslingers
For pens and microphones gripped between fingers
For the barrier breakers who showed   everyone   it **can** be done

For public communicators of private struggles
For lives reborn from rubble
For poets writing their way out of trouble

For every poem written that aides in resurrection
        or sparking insurrection
For every poet challenging convention
For all the witty epithets doubling as reactionary couplets

and for poets surprised by what they've created
For poets who make this look uncomplicated

For every journal kept hidden
For every instrumental or internal beat ridden
For every writer reaching for knowledge forgotten or forbidden
        on every stage and page graced with a verse that did not want
        but needed to be written

For every seasoned sage or first-timer
        faced with whatever it means to call yourself a writer
For every fabled poet spinning fables
For anyone under our sun shunning easy labels
For every poem in every language under Babel!

For the poets who are right with us
      from graveyard to cradle

For the poems that keep us stable

For the poets everywhere
and the poetry that got them there
                  round of applause please!
                  this is

For
    The
        Poets

Aretha and Grace

It was sound that saved a man like me

words whispered before new beginnings
are wayfaring songs between felt and unseen
implanted, sinewed and evergreen

certain silences unsettle me

like when an empty theatre's curtain swings
while serene and still the dusty stalls
appear surreal to the those enthralled
by the spirits starved of revelry

It was sound that saved a man like me

The Faithful

divine deep drum   meets   hallowed hall hum

where I two step
activate funk tech
and move
like
mech

be the automaton phenomenon

hear the guest emcee
her Hip Hop is what I be on
fan blade rap pace rhymes heavier than a jeep
vibing with orchestral chimes or monitor bleeps
when we few are gathered here it's a moment to keep

disused tunnels become reclaimed space
the best beat bangs in tightest embrace
hearts to hearts pound in the rumble of bass
escape is this place
is this state
is this beat   in these feet
syncopated
off-beat

these nights   these sights
exalted are these songs
bring your schmaltz
we can waltz
to hi-hats and gongs
and as the beat goes on and hits me with a lurch,
I sing
to the Faithful

this is our church and this is where we heal our hurts

I Haven't Written Honestly Since They Started Banning Drill

I hover pen over page   my insides knotted
Time to commit   engage   sign upon the dotted
whether at bliss   enraged   ideas fluid or solid
I begin by paying homage to those dishonored;

    the dispossessed, discriminated against, those detained illegally on islands
    the prisoners who dared to speak, risking being clapped in irons
    The First Nations, the Indigenous, Adivasi, Black, and aboriginal,

because our freedoms and privilege are maintained through this violence
because we stand on land polluted by greed and diamonds
please, a moment of silence.

My pen drops half an inch before I flinch and wrench it back

                        quick as a flash
I stew   thinking eventually the words will just descend on me
like the Lord descending to Daniel in the Lion's Den
or appearing to Nebuchadnezzar's imprisoned men
if I sit in a fiery furnace   convinced I'm the most truthful

                    and the most earnest
somehow these words will be my sermon

                    and reach the furthest
I can burn this fake fuel until the cows come home
be a song seeking salvation through short-sighted sycophants
I can bite back my tongue and protect my neck
from these wild situations

               but again   hesitation

I drop nib like a needle in a groove in lockstep bounded to my truth
but my hand won't flex and my pen won't move
blotting ink soaking the page like shirts man are shot in
hands off my voice and know the old style was rotten
now we kick rhymes in fields where we used to pick cotton
coughing in smoke relaying what life's like
residing in coffin blocks ten storeys high
still shotting out of bandos   don't ask me why
this message is encrypted and my tongue stay tied

A woman whose face curves like mine holds a bowl and mortar
in an A3 frame with an embossed paisley pattern
                     underneath her wrist is written
                     AKWAABA
syrup is spilling from the bowl
her knuckles point out into the room
mangled and shot with tension
battle-weary and beleaguered
and inviting me to pay my respects.

She's been pounding her fist so long I thought it was my heartbeat
grinding so long I forgot it was for my heart's peace

Sometimes she drops the pestle and mixes grain with her fingertips
sneaking in sweet fruit picked from fresh soil grown the old way
packing it in so high that the bowl runneth over
I cup my hands and drink
       spill nourishment all down my chin
            all over my pristine shirt and my ornamental hands
I dip my fingers in the mess and play

Swinging

I remember how we ran through trees and woods when we were kids
we used to dream of forests

I still wish for our four wrists interlocked in bliss
we could hide from tomorrow wrapped in a late night kiss
I would feel you next to me   after years of Friday nights in
only now I start to wonder   and the doubt settles in

I try to see around you   or over   or under   or through
but it's blatantly obvious   what I want to do   love you
and have done to me   love me
be serene with me   dream with me
be bereft of stress with me
it's been going since we were three
you helped start the spark in me
helped plant the seed
and we grew up and our affection spread out wide
grew into sprawling trees with branches seeking love
leafing through strangers in bookstores   who could be more
strangers on dancefloors   who could be more
people I'll never see again   but never saw before
thinking over and over   could be so, so much more

yet we come back to each other   and I've never been so sure
pure or impure   fact of the matter is   tonight our bodies might
soar and shake
we can live the life   in the dead of night   where voices quake
and we breakthrough

to see one another blooming
with a love all consuming
it will be no illusion
      Quiet the rage
      Quell the anger
      Satisfy the greed
      Remove the pride
      Uncover our eyes
and   just leave lust   just......

suddenly I'm awake and before I have time to calm myself down
the words have shot out of my mouth
          "Hey! Do you wanna be free with me?!"

you respond   hazily

           "what on earth are you on about?
           it's quarter past 3..."

what I had meant to say was
I want us to be free in love like we were free in childhood,
when deep down we believed that the world was all good,
before we let fret, sex, and debt define our beings
and all we cared about was see-sawing   monkey bars   and swinging

II

Despair & Desperation
(for DMX)

Once I Get Out Of Bed...

I will draw the day deep, be at peace with the world
ambling arm in arm with my love   living our best lives
strolling round museums and galleries
camping in Glastonbury fields
rambling through the tucked folds of metropoles
booking corner tables at rooftop restaurants and basement bars
sharing picturesque meals and speaking of everything earnestly
kissing like kids skipping school before striding out to the street

floating our way home
waiting up for the dawn chorus

awaking to whipping nightsticks
fists banging at the door
shriveling from revving tongues
reading glazed eyes sunk into cropped faces
hidden behind dirty visors and frosted glass

and we're begging in a single scorched voice
screeching holes out of the house
puckered into a corner
dying with the light of the morning

I pray in the street nightly ever sinc
burning memories and dreams into the pavement
I kneel with chalk and torch to talk of joys
that burnt me alive in their living

A Black View

I woke up to another set of terrorist threats
revealing seriously corrupted mindsets
Convinced me I might have to grab a bulletproof vest before my next test,
and to avoid challenging jokes   (no, not even in jest)
and not to speak too loud
it's dangerous to protest
just be happily repressed and under constant duress,
remember, it's always best to express

                       caution

While the world outside is storming
while praying for a peaceful dawning
while baying for one fine morning
to the sky I found myself calling
if I was in the wrong place wrong time, would it be my family mourning?
Would it be my body in the casket laid?
Would it prove worthy of adoring?
If my blood was still gently pouring out   as I was laying in the street
dead meat splayed out   and my mouth open wide like I'm yawning
would that image succeed in being flooring enough?
Would that portrait leave onlookers dumbstruck?
Could it serve as a black boy's warning?

"I'm sorry, the system wasn't built for you"
Send your complaints to whoever's not ignoring.

But if that injustice is still gnawing away
bottle up righteous rage for a rainy day
you'll need it when the horrors are thrown your way
through trials and pain, you'll feel what to say.

And as these words are sealed neatly in a coffin
and as the last light draws in
I beg you think of the state of things
of these biting winters
and mirages of spring

and of sins.

Desecrated

When Christ the Redeemer descends on Deptford High Street
only the rain will fall to wash his feet.

The kids will have already grown weary and tired of waiting.

When the Prince Of Peace has finished his late shift
the bus driver will miss him
huddleslumped against the shelter
                              and only three hours before the early start.

The Godhead made flesh again on Dalston Lane will break in private gardens.
The patrols around Gethsemane felt the same.

His Holiness, His Glorious Name will sing no song on the banks of the Thames
He will gag on London's waste at Beckton, choke at City Airport
and cackle at futility through the fumes.

After following the River Lea up to Tottenham
                              Yahweh will face matchday and divided loyalties.

The Lord Creator will be run out of the Barking, Brent, and Brixton Town halls
after the Council assessment found him to be fit for work but culturally
incompatible.

God will be judged in a trial held on the tube and sentenced to penance
sweeping the halls of St. Paul's.

They say cleanliness is next to godliness.

God has reconsidered what to polish, what to purify, what to burn.

Can't Stop Won't Stop

yes-yes   yes-yes
let's go   let's go
let's get it   let's get it
gotta move   gotta move
gotta stack that paper
gotta make that cheddar
gotta chase that bag
gotta get that bank!

Cash Rules Everything Around Me
bow down to the pound
don't stop don't stop
gotta hustle gotta juggle
gotta tightrope walk
more work less talk
and you better get yours
cos imma get mine
I'll be fine when I dead off this nine to nine
eight days a week at the standard grind
grinding out shifts
grinding coffee for the pricks

"Can I get a skinny wet decaf almond double flat white with a cinnamon twist?"

if you insist.

Don't push me.
I'm close to the edge

whatever the weather
whatever the method
it's all of my effort not to...

I'm doing ten toes
grindstone never left my nose
in this city
where you can't stop can't stop
can't breathe   can't breathe
no justice   no peace
no sobriety   no release
sleep no more for London hath murdered sleep

so we kick back   roll spliff
take a load off   get licked
before bliss slips to guilt trip
a quick blip
a rip   in   time
and back to the grind
I gotta make it, so I can't stop!

Coz when I'm there...
with my sweet hard earned freedom filling in the air
sniffing the glory   of the feast
I worked years to ensnare

I'll sit still
and wait
for the others

and the rest

Memoriam For A Fallen Pear

There's a pear tree in a graveyard.
I sent a prayer into its branches
tied around the sounds from my soul
and waited for fruit to fall.

I was still,
and hoping beyond hope.

With my back flat on the earth
I began stretching my pockets with
prayers sent up by other people.

Maybe they hadn't waited until the time was right
or they didn't know how to spot when a prayer is ripe or rotten.

I kept watch as long as I could.

Eventually my arms folded across my chest
head still towards the heavens,
sifting through the branches
awaiting my omen.

until I fell asleep

and fallen prayers rotted beside me.

Sick With Weight

Once, excavation rhymed with escapism
I'd dig for memories
immersed in earth
and echoing laughter
       listen for lost joy...

Now the door splinters open
and screws scatter
grief buried in the walls
despair in time capsules
spring loaded for me to find
with trembling lips and buzzing heart
ungrounded.

And I miss the one who blew blessings back home
blossomed glossy and wide
like mushrooming clouds
swam easy like starlings singing through sky

when celebration rose in harmony
even as the wailing Auntie
held my hand

       steal away little Lost Boy
       rub the dirt off your knees
       return home and be greeted
       and be at peace

III

Deep In The Belly Of The Beast
(For Benjamin Zephaniah and
Linton Kwesi Johnson)

Seeping

I am being drained.
Slowly, clinically.
Pierced at precious pressure points,
with holes jabbed into joints,
for ease of stain removal.

These pristine prime cuts, preserved for appetising presentation.

The process of this preparation persists like Sisyphus.

Slow globs spill and grow around my hanging body.

Punctured and pickled.

I am being picked apart.

Drip times drip
           over the time   it takes
                      for my body
                              to stop considering
                                    itself alive.

Heavy Footsteps In The Snow

Battle lines drawn across side streets
                                I can't tell if I'm crying from the chill.
Yutes convinced they're dealing out justice.
Step out of line, get beat.   Step   across   road.
                                Keep your eyes on your feet.

                I usually close my eyes but I wanted to see the churchyard
                                its ground all white with snow
my face froze as I saw a man's nose get broke
group of kids cracked him like a bad dad joke
with balled fists   and tight grips
around bats and bars.

        A car passed, the driver wielding an icy stare of disregard
                        likely thinking
        it's just dead men and screams of pain from sons who've already seen
                Daddy's name in a graveyard

                                my words slipped out from under me
                                feeling unprotected and unsafe
                                young people killing for

misplaced faith   or fame
or saving face
donning black balaclavas as fighting armour
a few were weeping with anger or terror
others shook where they stood
or laughed emptily.

Fear behind pale skin peeking out from behind black cloth.

I wrote my words in the deep snow around the man's head.

In the morning I stepped over the churchgate
my body numb and shivering
frozen fingers
fumbling with flowers
offering a few more words
for a grave
with a name
too familiar.

Tommy Builds A Cocktail

Tommy spied a sun-dried palm tree in an untouched garden
with crusty dark skin and cracks riddling
all along its side, weeping out of its shell
he aimed for a branch and down a coconut fell

it didn't implode on impact or split in his grip
he had to kick it along the cobblestone path
drag the shell across a pebble-dashed wall
and hook up the jet-powered sandblaster.
Even a parade of lawnmower wheelies couldn't shred it.

After the stalemate, Tommy retrained as a mercenary
        infiltration   demolitions   counter-insurgency
and busted the shell wide open   with a perfect salute

Tommy chopped lime with a ceremonial sword
mixed barrel-aged rum with mashed mint in a Boston glass
sliced pineapples and sprinkled four sugar-heaped spoonfuls on top
and throttled it all together
before straining out any not quite pulverized pulp.

Tommy piled on crushed ice from the fridge dispenser
raked the evidence behind the second shed
and added red rose petals from the
planter on the roadside of the main drive
to garnish.

What Does Black Power Mean?

At late-night-coursework-cramming o'clock
a white boy is firing me questions about Black Panther.
I tell him we've got to get to work.   I can't concentrate.
He suggests I stop burying my head in books.
I have a habit of horcruxing hope
searching for refractions of identities in histories
lives torn apart that delivered us to where we are.
I once read

> the problem of British history
> is that it happened overseas
> using Black bodies as fuel
> overseas Britannia ruled

He asks me what black power means
asks me why Black Friday is the shopping holiday
asks me why Black politicians lie too
asks me why Black people's pain is still commodified and sold
asks me why Black people still kill it on social media
asks me why Black people are still killed on social media
and reminds me when he says the n-word it's different
cos he says it with the -a   not the -er

> psyching myself up to respond I knot ropes of references around my point
> "Who are you? A panther!
> What you got? Soul!
> What you got? Love!
> What you got? Pride!
> and I see pride! I see power!
> I see a bad-ass mother who don't take no crap offa nobody!
> Who fights for rights by any means necessary!
> Who would rather die on his feet than live on his knees!

Living it loud!
Young, gifted, and Black! and proud!
Remember their hands can't hit what their eyes can't see,
and they don't see race, so they won't see you coming!
Meanwhile you're dropping a sly Wakandan salute to your little cousin
and knowing that tomorrow's not promised for anyone
revolution has come
time to pick up the gun

I heard The Last Poets say niggers are scared of revolution and I was not scared
I felt love when I heard Atta and Baldwin and Poitier say we are not niggers
nig-nogs, negroes, BAMEs, or coloureds
nor exotic darkies or freshie sambos.
We were always the majority
and we are beautifully and powerfully and perpetually
Black"

My response is to see Blackness as a revolution   Black music as revolutions
    Black ancestry as revolution   Black dancing in revolutions
Black cooking at the revolution   Black people weaving stories for fun, for
history, and for revolution

I tell the white boy that loving yourself while Black is an act of rebellion against
the system
I pull up a saved by the bell hooks meme to explain what the system is
(it's something about a materialist white supremacist capitalist heteropatriarchy
and I instruct him to look it up)

I proclaim that I love my Blackness, and he should too
and that we should get back to work.
It's almost a new dawn -
we best be ready.

Beware The Vicar's Daughter

Beware the vicar's daughter and her privileged supporters
Beware police dogs in the streets and her jack-booted enforcers
Beware the steely gaze of Cameron's chief deporter
Beware connections with the banks, probably already bought her

Beware the friendly side of her appearing on The One Show
Beware smiling imperialists all gung-ho on the down-low
Beware her snooper's charter and her slightly soulless laughter
Beware the toffs, their scorn and scoffs surely signal disaster

Beware the wealth of nations founded in exploitation
Tobacco, cotton, sugar industries built on enslavement
Beware of those restricting your access to education
Knowledge is power
Beware those who withhold information

Beware of bullshit peddlers repeating
                         strong and stable
                    Brexit means Brexit
dare to test it?
                         TRAITOR!
                    screams the Mail

Beware hysteric media sensationalising trivia
while the legacies of Orgreave, Grenfell, and the Biafra,
of Peterloo and Hillsborough, and all across diasporas
remain untold or undersold
erased from our shared history

The past is now, the future now
I've got no time for mystery

Beware of apathy, it smells like privilege to me
If we're sitting on the fence then we're not fighting to be free

So fight with me against the Tories and their vicar's daughter
and be more than an election voter or party supporter
Know your rights, admit your wrongs
It does matter who wins.
The fight is on!

The bout to rebuild "Britishness" begins…

A Step-By-Step Guide To Saving 'The British Dream'

First, remove all chocolate, leaving only a legally approved Dream bar.

Separate the blood and sweat of children from those famed satanic mills.

Overlook industrialised people-trafficking while cheering for Common-wealth.

Fumigate the haunted Houses of Parliament and the dusty halls of Westminster.

Flush out muddy complexity like dirt in the workings of your white goods.

Brush away inconvenient brownness staining sea-to-blood-soaked sea.

Sanitise histories with doctored textbooks and stolen traditions.

Painstakingly apply PVA glue to cracks in the floor while tectonic plates shift.

Bury the black spots under thick coats of white powder and white noise.

Exfoliate in a panicked frenzy.

Cauterise festering wounds.

Wipe clean the white conscience.

Never look back.

Never look in.

Let a white Jesus forgive you all your sins,

and please,

God save 'the British Dream.'

IV

Leaving Breadcrumbs
(For Ty)

One Black Lotus (For William Davidson)

you must not eat from the tree of the knowledge of good and evil...
when you eat from it you will certainly die. - Genesis 2:17

Birthed by a Black woman   dead stock
deemed unworthy to record   surplus produce
under the watch of man installed to inflict British justice on us
                                         just subjects

When shipped to Scotland for schooling
you dipped out and sought solace on the sea that was your exile.
Upon return and by demand, strong-armed to serve at sea for the crown
yet anchored enough in the law of the land to unionise and make a stand
to be a Black British man breaking bread in the badlands
from London to Liverpool to Birmingham;
a maker.
Building for the people
with his own hands

Then, with Peterloo as your witness
and eleven murdered, fighting for a voice
you hit the books to shame the crooks
preaching common ownership for the common cause

It was all for one and one for all before infiltration and downfall
a copper undercover seeded a tantalising thought

"Let's blow the government to hell in the style of Guy Fawkes!"

and before the ink had dried that scurrilous spy
sold you out for highest treason
divide and conquer works the same
from Cato Street, London to Jamaica in the Caribbean.

In court you challenged the judge

   "Would you rather not govern a country of spirited people than cowards?"

*

Our radical leaves are dissected   and pressed between pages

dead bodies like flowers   preserved for the ages   prematurely
cut.

I want my history blooming and rooted like a living tree
for it is ancient tradition
to resist fuckry.

The Cocoon Cracks From Outside

suddenly   at the break of day
woodcutters glided
they burned the grass
the roots   wrecked and shorn

lofty pilgrims crawled towards anguish
possessed by the rush to war

fires burst, limbs snapping
penetrating prayers

We were cut off from our surroundings   we could not understand
We were too far   and could not remember

the Motionless Man was cursing us   phantoms in a madhouse
on an unknown planet   sustained yells
incomprehensible

We struggled against the frenzy and fought   alone

Until the forest stepped in
all leisurely
beckoning us
with a mass of hands clapping
of feet stomping
of limbs swaying
of eyes
and eyes
and eyes all here

we rode away on the roll of the drums
leaving hardly a trace

(a found poem, using words taken from a single page of Joseph Conrad's
Heart Of Darkness*)*

Resurvival

(A Gimbal after Nii Ayikwei Parkes & Margaret Atwood)

They'll make believe we saved one single quill still sitting in its quiver
and let it stand so long the shills fell from its spine and withered
what was left intact will be corralled, compressed under a half-fist
and aimed up high, shot to the sky   hollow bones are an easier lift
weightless tales buffed blank and flung out with the sharpest barbs reburied

what of our remains survive alive and still giving?

under fire from mandatory nonsense and absurd diktats
we coalesce on calabash round cowrie shells caught from the kickback
and twang true in elastic funk bands, drum-rolling into waves
spread thin as morning mist, sprinkling rice dust laced with bass

what happens when we cannot bear it one day more?

when the cretinous creditors and their debts are ditched
bank's statements left ignored   the calls to arms dodged
we sanctify those they chose to slay   enact divestment en masse   refusal to pay
trust fall down that unknowable warren yet land on patterned pelts

which sacrifices will we mourn?

as our memorials are cannibalised and marched through factory warzones
wincing wings   restrained   under corrosive lights   ripped apart   alone
until the flock signalled the hour has come to fly across
and above the haunted shallow wharf   outside the range of crossfire

amass enough momentum   shed the weight   leave a trail

Discovering Poems Through Observation And Elimination

(after Nikki Giovanni)

THIS IS NOT A POEM
it's an outpouring of rage I've been swilling in my mind, over my tongue,
in between my teeth but never swallowing
THIS IS NOT A LIFE
said Nikki Giovanni
and history jumped two feet to the left, corrected itself,
said "sorry ma'am, my mistake"

THIS IS NOT A LIFE
because I'm not proud enough to be queer   or queer enough to be proud
never been to cabaret
can't pose right
don't sit right
won't dress right
faced with secret angles and angry clanging doors banged in my face because
THIS IS NOT A POEM
nor an open letter, court summons or civic address
it's not shielded by acts of Parliament, the will of the people, or market forces
THIS IS NOT A LIFE
because I can't be everywhere at once
being all things
to all people
at all times
on all platforms
in all languages
I know
THIS IS NOT A POEM

because it didn't get the grant
or get through Grantium
or get published in Granta
                    so THIS IS NOT A POEM
because I don't want to submit it   or submit to it
don't want to speak it   much less be spoken to by it
don't want to learn it   or learn from it
I'm ashamed to face it   because
                    THIS IS NOT A LIFE
and I am not a leader
I am not the solution scribed on a bullet
stuffed in a chamber sent to rip flesh and minds from slumber or stasis
I am not here for you
Me, myself and I and I are hunting for better living and working conditions
I am not giving you what you want
I am not limber but stiff and stubborn and   taught   and   tense   because
                    THIS IS NOT A LIFE
and we don't need poems to party   but they help
and we don't need poems to protest   but they help
and we don't need poems at funerals   but they help
and we don't need poems to speak   but they help
we just need poetry to be
so

THIS IS NOT A POEM   but you're doing fine
THIS IS NOT A POEM   and your life matters
THIS IS NOT A POEM   and we gon' be alright
THIS IS NOT A POEM   THIS IS NOT A PIPE   THIS IS NOT A DREAM

                    THIS IS NOT A PIPE
                    THIS IS NOT A DEATH
            THIS IS A MEMORY   THIS IS A PROPHECY
                    THIS IS A LIFE
                    and THAT IS A POEM

ACKNOWLEDGEMENTS:

To all of my family and friends who've loved and supported me up to
and through this moment,

To my crew at Pen-Ting Poetry, Boomerang, and Imaginary Millions,
where so many of these poems were born and sculpted into what's
been published here.

To the writing communities and collectives I've been a part of; the
Roundhouse Collective, Obsidian Foundation (Group E) and The
Writing Room.

To my tutors, including Bridget Minamore, Cecilia Knapp, Zena
Edwards, Roger Robinson, Malika Booker, Terrance Hayes, Dante Mi-
cheaux, Nick Makoha, Raymond Antrobus, and Zena Edwards.

To Sylvia Arthur at the Library of the Africa + The African Diaspora
and Sharon Fulton at Clean Prose,

To Lisa Mead and Apples & Snakes,

To every poetry night that's ever booked me,

To the audience members, readers, and listeners who continue to
spend time with me,

To the poets and proofreaders who guided the book through each of
its embryonic phases and gave me editing advice, counsel and
encouragement,

And to all those who've helped me along the way that I've not
mentioned, know that I am grateful for the support - whoever and
wherever you may be, whenever and however you've supported me.

Thank you.

ABOUT THE AUTHOR:

Peter deGraft-Johnson is The Repeat Beat Poet, a Hip Hop writer and broadcaster working to capture and extend moments of time, thought, and feeling. Peter, a British-born Ghanaian has performed across the UK and internationally at venues including the Southbank Centre and Ronnie Scotts in London, alongside writers like Margaret Atwood, Salena Godden (FRSL) and Roger Robinson (TS Eliot Prize).

Peter is the co-founder of leading Hip Hop open mic night Pen-Ting, a host of longstanding cornerstone London poetry open mic Boomerang and a house emcee with Hip Hop label, jam night and radio show Imaginary Millions. Peter also presents his monthly radio show #TheRepeatBeatBroadcast and since 2021 has hosted the multi-award nominated Lunar Poetry Podcast, which is archived in the British Library.

Peter has been nominated for a Jerwood Compton Poetry Fellowship, selected by BBC 1Xtra and the Roundhouse for their Poetry Collective programmes, is an Obsidian Foundation fellow and has produced work in collaboration with The UN and the London School of Economics for COP26 with the Hot Poets anthology. His work has been published by Magma Poetry, Bad Betty Press and Poetry On The Picket Line and in 2021 he was an inaugural writer-in-residence at the Library of Africa & The African Diaspora in Accra, Ghana.

His debut single *This That* was released in 2020 to rave reviews. He is a regular at jam sessions across London, hosting and working with leading lights of London's nu jazz scene like Steam Down and Jelly Cleaver and contributing poetry to the cinematic jazz project Silvertongue for their debut album *Beneath The Surface*. In 2021 he opened for Ghanaian multi-instrumentalist Kwame Yeboah, appeared with Fela Kuti's longtime saxophonist Bukky Leo and was accompanied on stage by modern bass virtuoso Thundercat.

Peter hosts and facilitates poetry workshops in schools, medical settings and drama groups. He has also written film and arts journalism, with bylines in TimeOut London, The BFI, The Prince Charles Cinema, and is a co-ordinator for the Chelmsford Film Festival.

POEM CREDITS:

Beware The Vicar's Daughter (video by Muddy Feet Poetry, online)
One Black Lotus (For William Davidson) (video by Muddy Feet Poetry, online)
For The Poets + The Faithful (video by Apples + Snakes, online)

For The Poets, *Elephant Journal* (2018, online)

I Haven't Written Honestly Since They Started Banning Drill was originally commissioned for the Words That Burn campaign by Amnesty International. (2019, online)

Seeping appears in the *Alter Egos anthology* by Bad Betty Press (2019) and on the Southbank Centre's Instagram (2020)

Desecrated was aired on BBC Radio London. (2020)

Sick With Weight appears in *Magma Poetry #77 - Act Your Age* (2020)

Cocoon Cracks From The Outside appears in the *I Know I Wish I Will* anthology by Eastside (2020)

Resurvival was originally commissioned by Apples & Snakes, in response to Margaret Atwood's poem Feather from *Dearly* (2020).

What Does Black Power Mean? appears in *The Black Anthology: Language*. 10:10 Press. (2021)

OTHER WORKS BY THE AUTHOR:

Music

The Repeat Beat Poet - This That, ft. SafeNath (single)

Imaginary Millions - The Faithful (ft. RBP)
Silvertongue - Beneath The Surface (album). (featured on Epics Of
Humanity and Ghana)
Jelly Cleaver - It's A Madness (ft. RBP)
The Repeat Beat Poet & Danny Drive Thru - Cocoon Cracks

Broadcasting

The Lunar Poetry Podcast - A longform interview podcast,
investigating the worlds of those who weave magic with words.
Archived in the British Library, Sounds Department.
https://lunarpoetrypodcasts.com/

Why Poetry? The Lunary Poetry Anthology Vol. 1 also available on
Verve Poetry Press.

#RepeatBeatBroadcast - the monthly audio voyage guided by the
Repeat Beat Poet, archived on Threads Radio's Mixcloud page.
https://www.mixcloud.com/ThreadsRadio/playlists/the-repeat-beat-
broadcast/

ABOUT VERVE POETRY PRESS

Verve Poetry Press is a quite new and already award-winning press that focussed initially on meeting a local need in Birmingham - a need for the vibrant poetry scene here in Brum to find a way to present itself to the poetry world via publication. Co-founded by Stuart Bartholomew and Amerah Saleh, it now publishes poets from all corners of the UK and beyond - poets that speak to the city's varied and energetic qualities and will contribute to its many poetic stories.

Added to this is a colourful pamphlet series, many featuring poets who have performed at our sister festival - and a poetry show series which captures the magic of longer poetry performance pieces by festival alumni such as Polarbear, Matt Abbott and Genevieve Carver.

The press has been voted Most Innovative Publisher at the Saboteur Awards, and has won the Publisher's Award for Poetry Pamphlets at the Michael Marks Awards.

Like the festival, we strive to think about poetry in inclusive ways and embrace the multiplicity of approaches towards this glorious art.

www.vervepoetrypress.com
@VervePoetryPres
mail@vervepoetrypress.com